SUDDENLY A
Centerpiece

SUDDENLY A
Centerpiece

ASSEMBLE THESE CLEVER TABLE DESIGNS
IN NO TIME AT ALL

SHER SIMON

CREATIVE
PUBLISHING
international

CHANHASSEN, MINNESOTA

Copyright © 2005
Creative Publishing international, Inc.
18705 Lake Drive East
Chanhassen, Minnesota 55317
1-800-328-3895
www.creativepub.com
All rights reserved

Vice President/Publisher: Linda Ball
Vice President/Retail Sales: Kevin Haas

Executive Editor: Alison Brown Cerier
Managing Editor: Yen Le
Art Direction/Design: Lois Stanfield
Senior Editor: Linda Neubauer
Photo Stylist: Joanne Wawra
Director of Production and Photography: Kim Gerber

Photographer: John Abernathy
Copy Editor: Donna Hoel

Library of Congress Cataloging-in-Publication Data

Simon, Sher.
  Suddenly a centerpiece : assemble these clever table
designs in no time at all / by Sher Simon.
       p. cm.
  Includes index.
  ISBN 1-58923-170-8 (soft cover)
  1. Centerpieces. 2. Handicraft. I. Title.
  TX879.S35 2004
  642'.8--dc22

                                    2004014958

Printed by RR Donnelley:
10 9 8 7 6 5 4 3 2 1

Photo: Lisa Thies

S HER SIMON, a leading expert on home accessories and faux floral design, is a floral designer and consultant to home furnishing stores and private clients. Her popular how-to seminars showcasing trends in accessories and florals have inspired thousands of people to be creative. She has also appeared monthly on a morning television program to present seasonal looks.

Sher has worked with the most upscale accessories and floral products, but she also loves a good bargain. She knows how to make something from the clearance rack look like a million bucks, and she finds elements for her designs everywhere from the supermarket to garage sales. She encourages people to use what they have at home, to experiment, and to have fun!

Sher lives with her family in Minneapolis, Minnesota.

The author would like to thank Gabberts Furniture and Design Studio for its support, with special thanks to Rose Larsen and Brian Grogan for all their help.

Contents

A Little of This, A Little of That

Acenterpiece can bring the season of the year or the heart of a celebration to your table. It can spark the conversation at a dinner party or make a holiday meal a bit more special. When friends and family gather, a centerpiece is in many ways at the center of it all.

Yet who has hours to spend crafting a centerpiece? I certainly don't, especially when I'm hosting and need to cook, clean, and get ready. With time at a premium, it's easy to understand why the people who attend my floral seminars get the most excited about the quick and easy ideas.

In this book, you'll find original centerpieces that anyone can assemble quickly and easily. A little of this, a little of that, and suddenly you will have a centerpiece!

The book has two sections. The first section includes centerpieces for decorating your dining table for the seasons of the year. These designs can be used for many months, bringing the colors, florals, and overall feel of the season to your table.

The centerpieces in the second group are designed for a wide variety of occasions, from a romantic dinner for two to a beach party in the backyard. Included are centerpieces that reflect the menu, such as Asian or south of the border, as well as designs for holiday meals. Some of these designs use fresh vegetables or flowers. Feel free to choose something from group one for entertaining or group two for enhancing your décor.

In fact, feeling free is what my approach to design is all about. I'm hoping you'll find inspiration in these designs and then make them your own. Don't worry about technique—the ideas in this book are easy and don't require crafting skill. Don't worry about the "rules" of design—just be creative and have fun.

Before you pick a project and get started, here are some useful tips on designing centerpieces and choosing the materials used to make them.

Tips on Centerpieces

- If you want people to converse across the table, keep the centerpiece low. Centerpieces that are tall or broad often have to be removed as soon as the meal starts, leaving an empty space in the middle of the table. A large centerpiece is perfect for buffet serving or for a table that is rarely used, but otherwise, think low.

- Make sure that the centerpiece leaves enough room for the place settings and serving pieces. It helps to set the table and try out the centerpiece for size before you finish it.

- A centerpiece should look good from every seat at the table. Move around the design as you're assembling it, checking out the view from different angles.

- The centerpiece should complement the style and colors of the room, china, and linens. However, the colors need not match completely; often a different color makes the look pop.

- On a practical level, if you will be using the centerpiece for awhile, it should be easily movable.

- Loose, asymmetrical designs feel more comfortable and are more sophisticated. Rumple the fabrics, avoid straight lines, tie a floppy bow. Choose odd numbers of items—three, five, seven.

- Above all, think about the mood you want to create: elegant, dramatic, soothing, fun, or festive.

Tips on Faux Florals

- Faux (often called silk) flowers are long-lasting and don't need tending. People with allergies appreciate them, too. Many faux flowers look amazingly real and are popular for home decorating.

- Since the florals will be seen up close, it is important to get the best quality. Look for botanically correct florals with vibrant colors and natural-looking stems and leaves. Many designs in this book use only a few floral elements, so you can afford to buy the best.

- Before using the florals, fluff the flower heads and shape the leaves. Stretch out faux evergreen stems and garlands until they look like fresh ones.

- Faux floral designs use dry floral foam, which is different from the foam used for fresh flowers. This firm, gray or green foam comes in blocks and 2" (5 cm) sheets. You can cut it with a utility knife. I've found that a metal putty knife cuts foam quickly and easily, too. Then you can trim the edges with a sharper knife.

- While floral designers usually glue faux flowers in place, you can often just insert them into foam, rock, or other fillers without bothering to glue. Not only do you save work, but you can change the florals easily to take the design into a new season. Often you can leave the stems long; they can be curled under inside a vase, and sometimes they become part of the design.

- If you won't be reusing the container, you can glue the foam into it. Otherwise, use this trick. Put duct tape on the bottom of the container, then glue the foam to the duct tape. When you're ready to reuse the container, just peel off the tape.

Tips on Fresh Flowers

- Fresh flowers are wonderful but they don't last forever. Many designs can be made with either faux or fresh flowers.

- Be sure to use floral preservative in the water. The flowers will last much longer. Also, cut the stems at an angle so they can soak up as much water as possible.

- Insert single stems into water tubes to keep them fresh longer.

- Foam for fresh flowers is designed to soak up and hold lots of water. To use fresh floral foam, cut it to the desired shape and place it in fresh water that contains floral preservative. Let the foam soak up the water at its own pace; don't push it down into the water or air bubbles can form. Then secure the foam into your container using waterproof tape.

- If you are using a decorative container that is not waterproof, place a plastic liner into it before adding the wet foam.

- After inserting the flowers, cover any exposed foam with moss.

Tips on Containers and Accessories

- The designs in this book include a wide range of home accessories, china, and collectables. A centerpiece can be built around anything from a vintage coffee can to a silver champagne bucket. A galvanized sand bucket, an heirloom tureen, or a ceramic pasta bowl can find its way to the center of your table. So look around your home and see what you already have.

- Garage sales and flea markets are great places to shop for containers of all kinds.

- Bring your container along when you purchase flowers to help you choose the right size and quantity.

- Weight a container with rocks or sand if it is tippy.

- Consider new ways to use your accessories. For example, an upside-down cake stand can be a candle holder.

Tips on Candles and Candlesticks

- Many centerpieces include candles, for good reasons. The soft light of candles does a lot to create the right mood. It helps the table—and the people seated around it—look better!

- **Important**: Make sure that florals, ribbon, and other elements are a safe distance from the candle flame. Never leave burning candles unattended.

- Taper candles (tall and slender) are available in several lengths and are generally more formal than pillar candles (the chunky ones). Pillars come in a wide range of styles and sizes. They last longer than tapers and give your arrangement a casual look.

- Choose candles to complement the candleholder and the whole arrangement. The size and shape should be right for the holder. Take your candleholders to the store when you buy candles to be sure you get the right size.

- Solid-color candles go well with busy, multicolor arrangements. Candles with colorful embellishments add interest to simple arrangements, like leafy garlands or plain table wreaths.

- If you have a long, rectangular table, put candlesticks off to the sides to extend the centerpiece.

- Secure candles in a holder with a bit of candle adhesive, sold in small tins.

- Floating candles are inexpensive and can be changed often. Play with different colors to coordinate with the seasons. Float fresh flower heads with the candles and add ribbon for a festive look. Before adding water, cover the bottom of the floating candle container with creative fillers, such as rocks, marbles, beads, sand, or heavy seashells.

- Candles burn best if you trim the wicks to $1/4$" (6 mm).

- If the candle is too wide for the holder, you can trim the bottom with your scissors or a knife.

- Votive holders are small glass or metal containers that hold short candles or tea lights. Votive candles burn quickly and can be changed often to suit the design. Filled glass votives are candles that are poured directly into the holder and are not removable.

Tips on Table Linens

- The color of the tablecloth, placemats, or runner should complement the colors of the room. A cream or white tablecloth works in most rooms. You may want to choose a lively color for a special occasion or dinner party. If the linens are bright, make sure they coordinate well with the container or other main elements of the centerpiece.

- If your centerpiece has a multicolor container, keep the florals in one color family. Plain containers are better for multicolor floral arrangements.

- Use a single-color fabric or table runner under a busy centerpiece. Or spice up a monochromatic centerpiece by placing a patterned or multicolor fabric under it.

- Consider the linens you already have before going off to buy something for an occasion. The centerpiece often is the focal point, rather than the linens under it.

- Many centerpieces include a runner, which sets off the other elements and helps hold the piece together. I like to scrunch up a runner for a looser look.

- A gorgeous throw or scarf arranged in a swirl or softly gathered adds a sophisticated element under a centerpiece.

- Fabric stores are another resource for materials or special accents for your arrangement.

Tips on Craft Materials

- Craft stores sell a variety of fillers for containers: decorative rocks, sand, dried pods, and so on. These greatly enhance your centerpieces and can be used over and over.

- You can use either a glue gun or a glue pan for the times when you need to glue elements in your centerpiece. The gun puts the glue right where you want it, but be careful so you don't burn yourself. With the glue pan, you can dip stems and other items right into the glue. If you keep the pot on low, you won't get burned.

- Wire is used in many of the projects. Although there are many different gauges and types, 24-gauge wire works most of the time. You can always add an extra wire if you need more strength. Buy the wire in pieces at your craft store.

- Floral tape is a narrow strip of crepe paper coated with wax. It can be wrapped around wire to give a finished look. It's also used to join a wire to a faux floral stem to make it longer. Just wrap the tape around the wire or stem, stretching it slightly and using the heat of your fingers to soften the wax and seal it to the surface. The tape usually is available in brown and in light and dark green.

- Wood floral picks are used to attach faux fruits to a design and to extend stems.

- Cable ties from the hardware store do a good job of holding thick floral stems or evergreens together. The ties can be hidden by gluing on a bit of moss or a leaf.

- Ribbon adds elegance to a centerpiece and can create a special seasonal look. There are many wonderful choices available by the yard or spool at craft and fabric stores. Drape ribbon luxuriously through a garland or make simple floppy bows (below) and insert them wherever accents are needed.

Tying a Floppy Bow

1 Cut a 9" (23 cm) piece of wire and fold it into a U shape; set aside. Cut a 45" (115 cm) length of ribbon, angling the ends.

2 Drape the ribbon over your right index finger about 10" (25.5 cm) from one end, with the short tail toward you. Hold it in place with your thumb.

3 With your left hand, grasp the longer tail even with the short tail, raise it to your right hand, and hold in place behind the upper layer, forming a 5" (12.7 cm) loop.

4 Grasp the longer tail again, about 2" (5 cm) below the short tail, raise it to your right hand, and hold it in place, forming a second, slightly longer loop.

5 Twist the four layers together at the base of the loops, and wrap them tightly with the wire. Leave the wire ends long. Shake out the bow and adjust the loops and tails as desired.

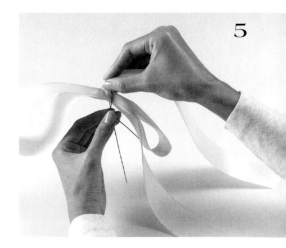

Seasonal Decorating

A Calming Center

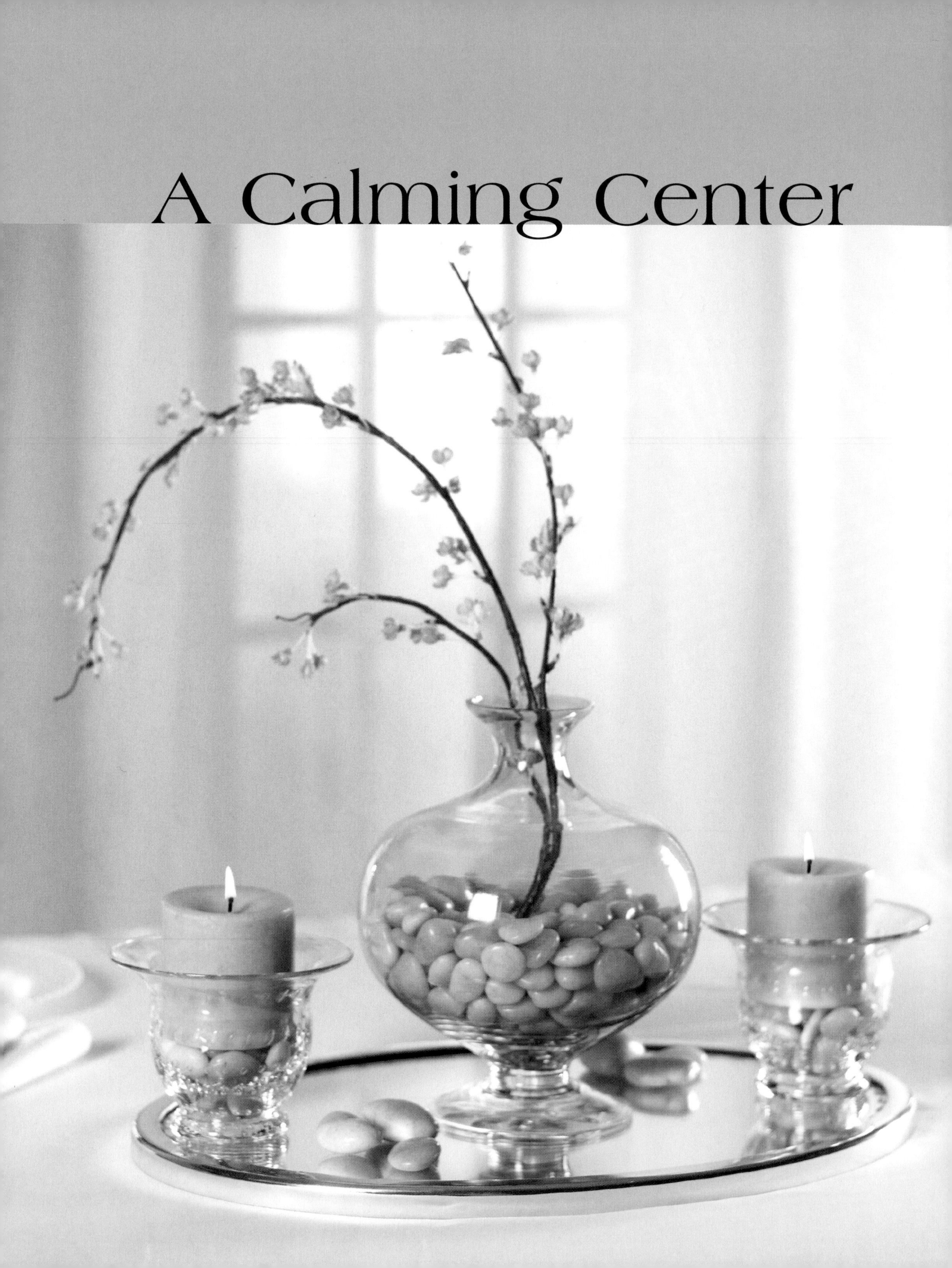

CHERRY BLOSSOM WITH RIVER ROCKS

This design creates a peaceful setting for a meal. Simple and clean, it combines soothing pale blues with one delicate branch of cherry blossoms. The cream-colored river rocks, sometimes called Zen stones, tie the design together; they are used inside the vase, in the candleholders, and scattered on the mirrored base.

A mirror is a wonderful base for a centerpiece because it reflects and magnifies candlelight. Mirrored wall hangings sold as "glass art" can be used as a base for an elegant centerpiece for a dinner party or holiday celebration. An inexpensive unframed mirror or a mirror from your own wall also work well for centerpieces.

A vase with a narrow, flared opening is a good choice for arrangements that use a single stem. Make sure you can pass the rocks through the opening. The candleholders are actually small, round vases.

ELEMENTS

Mirror or "glass art"

Clear glass vase about 12" (30.5 cm) tall

3-lb. (1350 g) bag medium-sized, white, river rocks

One stem faux cherry blossoms, 18" (46 cm) long

Two clear glass, round vases wide enough to hold the candles, 4" to 6" (10 to 15 cm) tall

Two short pillar candles

PUTTING IT TOGETHER

1 Position the mirror in the center of your table. Place the large vase in the center of the mirror and a small vase on each side.

2 Wash the rocks and allow them to dry. Set aside six of the larger ones.

3 Tip the vase and slide in the rocks, being careful not to break the glass, until you have several inches of rock at the bottom of the vase.

4

5

- Substitute another long, airy stem such as pussy willow or forsythia.

- Use fresh flowers and add water and floral preservative to the vase. Be careful not to damage the stems when you place them between the rocks.

- Change the colors, matching the candles to the vase; keep the colors pale and soothing.

- Move the design into fall by adding a few long pheasant feathers; the brown and blue look good together.

4   Determine how long you want the cherry blossom stem to be by holding it next to the container and bending up the end of the stem. If you need more height, you can re-bend the stem. Cut the stem and anchor it in the rocks. Gracefully arch the branch.

5   Fill the small vases with rocks until the candles extend about an inch above the rim. Insert the candles. Position the candleholders as shown.

6   Place the reserved rocks in groups of three on the glass mirror to tie it all together.

Wreathed Bowl

CLEAN DESIGN ON A RICE WREATH

Buy a classic white ceramic mixing bowl or pasta bowl or pull one out of your kitchen cabinet. Fill the bowl with one type of dried or faux vegetable or fruit and set it on a vibrantly colored rice wreath to make it pop. This small, self-contained, sturdy, family-friendly center-piece works well in a kitchen or casual dining area.

Match the produce to the color of the wreath for a calm, harmonious look. White porcelain looks very fresh against a green rice wreath and dried artichokes. Both the artichokes and the wreath add interesting textures, too.

When you buy the wreath, take the bowl with you to be sure it will cover the opening. The wreath needs a flat back so it rests evenly on the table.

ELEMENTS

Generously sized white bowl, such as a pasta bowl

Flat candle dish (won't be seen)

River rocks, about a pound (450 g)

Pillar candle

Rice wreath

Dried artichokes or faux fruits or vegetables

PUTTING IT TOGETHER

1   Put the wreath in the middle of your table. Set the bowl on top.

2   Place the candle dish and candle in the middle of the bowl. Add rocks to weight the bowl and keep the candle in place.

3   Fill the bowl with artichokes.

VARIATION Here's another unusual way to include a wreath in a centerpiece. Flip your cake stand over to make a candle holder. Twist stems of faux peonies together to form a loose ring. Place the peony ring over the inverted cake stand and insert a candle that matches your peonies. This is so simple but so fresh for spring and summer.

ADAPTATIONS

- Pears and clusters of green grapes can be used for variety.

- For a fall look, fill the bowl with decorative gourds.

- For the holidays, use a red rice wreath and fill the bowl with fresh or dried cranberries.

- Use seasonal fresh fruit.

- Choose a simple ivy wreath, a berry wreath, or a one-color floral wreath for a different look.

Wild Grasses

ZINNIAS WITH GALVANIZED TIN

This fresh, airy, energizing arrangement suits French country or transitional décor. Galvanized tin pans are wonderful containers for bright red flowers. Using flowers in all one color makes a strong statement. The container in the photograph is an antique tin dough riser, which has been in my collection for many years. The container won't be harmed by this arrangement because the flowers are set in a plastic liner and nothing is glued to the pan.

A round container like this one works especially well on a round table. Choose a container that allows room for the place settings but isn't dwarfed by the table.

Wild grasses are sold on the stem in craft stores. A kiwi green color sets off the red flowers beautifully, but many other colors are available.

ELEMENTS

Plastic liner that fits into the bottom of the container

Sheet of dry floral foam, 2" (5 cm) thick

Florist knife or utility knife

Glue gun

Vintage tin baking pan

A dozen long-stemmed faux zinnias

Wire cutters

Three bunches faux wild grass

PUTTING IT TOGETHER

1   Place the foam on a work surface and put the plastic liner on top of it. Using a marker, draw around the liner. Cut out the foam circle.

2   Glue the foam into the liner, using a ring of hot glue.

3   Cut the zinnia stems about 14" (35.5 cm) long with wire cutters. Bend and twist them until they look natural. Then insert the zinnias in the foam, leaving enough room for the grasses. Be careful that the arrangement doesn't look crowded.

4   Place the liner into the tin container. Insert the three bunches of grass in different places to balance the arrangement and fill in around the zinnias. Shorten the grass stems if they are too long.

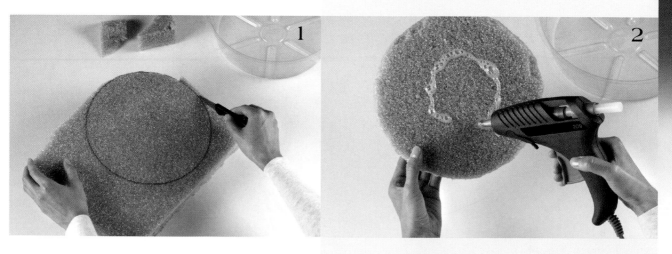

3

ADAPTATIONS

• Look for interesting vintage bakeware in antique stores.

• A turkey roasting pan would work great for a large table.

• Choose another bright flower in a single color; tulips or sunflowers are just two of the possibilities.

Vintage
Coffee Cans

COLLECTABLES

Wake up and smell the coffee! Browse through antique shops and you'll find many wonderful old tin food containers, especially coffee cans. Tin trays with bright painted designs are also easy to find. These are wonderful elements for a charming centerpiece for your kitchen table or casual dining area. Play with different possibilities before you buy, as you want to find cans that fill the tray.

On a practical level, a centerpiece on a tray is easily moved when the whole table surface is needed for homework, crafts, or paperwork. A small, clean arrangement like this is all you need in a busy kitchen.

Appropriately enough, the coffee cans are filled with coffee beans, whose aroma welcomes you into the kitchen every morning. Plain white pillar candles work well, but the decorative ones shown here add a floral touch to the design.

ELEMENTS

Vintage painted tin tray

Three small tin
coffee cans

2 lb. (1 kg) coffee
beans

Three pillar candles

PUTTING IT TOGETHER

1   Set the coffee cans on the tray.

2   Fill the cans three-quarters full with
    coffee beans.

3   Wiggle the candles about 2" (5 cm)
    into the coffee beans, until they feel
    secure and look the right height.

ADAPTATIONS

- Replace the candles with three small potted geraniums.

- Other possibilities for fillers are dry beans or elbow macaroni.

- Replace a candle with a small glass vase of fresh flowers. Choose something friendly and bright, such as gerbera daisies.

- Other possibilities for tin cans are biscuit tins and nut tins. (Don't use paper food packages that could catch fire.)

BRIGHTS ON ICE

When the weather gets hot, ice down your table with this centerpiece. Start by taking out that glass cake stand that you rarely use. (If you don't have one, keep an eye out at garage sales, as they are often found there.) Stack a smaller clear or nobnail pedestal candy dish on top.

The "ice cubes" are clear glass rocks, found at gardening or craft stores. The cake stand is covered with brightly colored potpourri from a craft store. Choose a chunky potpourri that includes elements such as dried pepperberries and whole flower heads. If the scent seems strong when you open the bag, let it air a bit before placing it on your dining table. The faux apple slices are optional, but fun. Craft stores sell them. This design comes together quickly and simply, leaving you time to sit and enjoy the sunset.

ELEMENTS

Glass cake stand

Small glass candy dish with a pedestal

Bag of potpourri

Pillar candle in a color that complements the potpourri, 5" (12.7 cm) tall

Clear glass rocks, about 3 lb. (1350 g)

Faux apple slices

PUTTING IT TOGETHER

1   Place the cake stand in the middle of your table. Place the small pedestal dish on top.

2   Cover the cake stand with potpourri.

3   Center the candle on the candy dish.

4   Place a ring of apple slices around the candle.

5   Use the clear rocks to fill in around the apple slices.

6   Pile rocks on the table—either around the base of the cake stand (for a round table) or extended to the sides (for a rectangular table).

2

5

6

ADAPTATIONS

- Use sliced dried oranges or artificial kiwi instead of the apple slices.

- For fresh flowers, line the candy dish with sheet moss. Cut fresh floral foam to size and soak it in water for a few minutes; place the foam on the moss. Cut flower stems about 4" (10 cm) long, and insert them into the foam, forming a rounded mass.

- For fall, use potpourri in autumn colors and accents such as leaves. Add a candle to match.

- In winter, switch to pine potpourri and a fresh, seasonal candle.

- Use clear glass cake stands for an elegant buffet table design. Stack them two by two, and place glass vases holding white roses among them.

Layers in Glass

FASCINATING FILLS FOR VASES, BOWLS, OR CANDLESTICKS

You can create eye-catching centerpieces by pouring layers of dried or fresh fillers into clear glass vases, bowls, or hollow candlesticks. An incredible variety of fillers is now sold by the bag. See the adaptations listed on page 41 for lots of ideas. You can switch the fillings to match the colors of the season. The fillings shown are perfect for fall.

Dress up the candlesticks or vases with a loose bow of satin ribbon. It's simple, but so elegant!

ELEMENTS

A pair of clear glass vases, bowls, or hollow candlesticks, about 12" (30.5 cm) tall

Two dried fillers in seasonal colors (shown here are tiny pinecones and dried pumpkin pods)

2 yd. (1.85 m) satin ribbon

Scissors

Two pillar candles

PUTTING IT TOGETHER

1   Pour the first filler into the containers until each is half full.

2   Pour in the second filler until the containers are full.

3   Cut the ribbon in half. Tie a "shoelace style" bow around the bottom of each container.

4   Place the candles on top of the containers.

VARIATION Make a quick centerpiece from a group of related decorative accents. Choose three containers, vases, candlesticks, or other objects that are different but have the same color and a related style. Each should be a different height; varying by two or three inches is ideal. Add a dried filler to one container, if you like. The grouping shown uses three elegant Roman-style accessories in ruby red and gold.

ADAPTATIONS

- Use fresh cranberries, sliced lemons or oranges (or both), kumquats, or other fruits with water.

- Fill a large glass container with red and green apples, fill with water, and add branches with leaves or flowers.

- Other fillers include green amra pods, rocks of various colors and types, gravel, dried beans, noodles in different colors and shapes, dried bamboo shoots, moss, and juniper berries.

Candelabra
Flourishes

SIMPLE ELEGANCE WITH BOWS AND BERRIES

A candelabra can be a grand centerpiece with just a few embellishments, such as wide ribbon and preserved greens. Choose colors that complement the style and color of your candelabra. The burnished blue-gray of this country French piece is set off by dark blue berries and cream-colored ribbon. Buy wide ribbon and tie a generous, abundant bow.

You can extend the arrangement with a bunched patterned tablecloth. This design also looks nice on an oak or whitewashed pine table.

A single candelabra is enough on a standard round table. If you have a long oblong or rectangular table, you could add a second candelabra. Use a piece of pottery in the middle for balance, and add faux or fresh grapes and fruit into the bowl.

Package preserved
greens with berries
(Hedera Arborea Berry
was used)

Wire cutters

2½ yd. (2.3 m) satin
ribbon, 2" (5 cm) wide

Scissors

Two 9" (23 cm) pieces
of 24-gauge floral wire

Candelabra

Small tablecloth, if
desired

Taper candles

PUTTING IT TOGETHER

1   Cut the berries into stems about
    4" (10 cm) long, using the wire cutters.
    Make two small bunches by wrapping
    several stems together with floral
    wire. Set the bunches aside.

2   Cut the ribbon in half. Make two
    bows following the instructions on
    page 12. Catch a berry bundle into
    each bow as you twist the wire.
    Leave the wire ends long.

1

3   Attach the bows and berries to the candelabra as shown, then wrap the wire around the candelabra and hide it with a leaf.

4   Arrange a tablecloth in the middle of the table, if desired.

5   Place the candelabra in the center of the table. Add the candles.

3

ADAPTATIONS

- An ivy garland can be twisted loosely around a candelabra, leaving enough greenery at the end to drape onto your table.

- A silver candelabra is beautiful with red ribbon and evergreen sprigs.

- A gold candelabra looks rich with sheer copper ribbon and beaded grapes.

Tuscan
Fruits and Wine

FRUITS IN POTTERY

Bring the warmth and abundance of Tuscany to your table with this lasting fruit arrangement. The faux grapes and fruits are wonderfully realistic. You can buy them already on wooden picks (look for long ones) or add picks yourself. Choose fruits in a variety of shapes and sizes to make an interesting grouping, but stay in the same rich, warm color family of gold, plum, and green. Include some fruits with leaves, if you can, to add interest. The exact number of fruits you need depends on the size of the container. For this old-world style use a rustic pottery container.

At the top, you can insert a small wine bottle to hold a candle. (Look for an Italian wine.) Set the bowl on a platter or use a swatch of bright fabric under the container to add interest, texture, and color.

ELEMENTS

Pottery container

Sheet of dry floral foam, 2" (5 cm) thick

Putty knife

Duct tape

Glue gun

Block of dry floral foam

Knife

Small empty wine bottle, about 9" (23 cm) tall

Several bunches of faux grapes in green and plum

Several kinds of faux fruits on long wood picks (pomegranates, apples, pears)

Wood picks, an awl , and floral tape if the fruit is not already on picks

Taper candle, 12" (30.5 cm) tall, in a color that complements the fruit and the bottle

PUTTING IT TOGETHER

1   Cut the sheet foam to fill the container completely from side to side, using a putty knife.

2   Stick duct tape on the bottom of the container. Glue the sheet foam to the duct tape.

3   Cut a 4" (10 cm) square of the block foam. Glue it to the top center of the sheet foam.

4   Place the wine bottle on top of the foam block and draw around it. Cut a hole in the foam about 1" (2.5 cm) deep; scoop out the foam with a spoon. Glue the bottle into the hole.

5   Place sheet moss over the foam and around the bottom of the bottle.

4

6　If the fruits are not already on picks, make a small hole in the fruit with an awl, and then glue in a wood pick.

7　If the fruits have picks but the picks aren't long enough, lengthen them by wrapping the pick together with another pick, using floral tape.

8　Add the grapes and other fruits, starting along the edge of the container and dangling grapes off the side. Work toward the middle, varying the height and colors of fruits and creating an abundant look.

9　Cut the candle in half. Place the top half in the wine bottle. Light the lower half, and use it to drip wax over the candle and bottle.

ADAPTATION

* For a similar but simpler look, place a pillar candle and candle-holder in the middle of a platter, then pile fruits on the platter. Tuscan-style pottery works well, as does a plain white platter.

Harvest Bowl

WITH AIRY ACCENTS AND A SHAWL

A bowl of fruit is a popular everyday centerpiece, but a plain one is a bit dull. You can transform the look by placing the bowl on a richly patterned shawl and adding some fall berry stems. This warm, casual design takes you from harvest to holidays.

Start with a rustic wooden bowl filled with the glowing reds and golds of faux pomegranates and mangoes. Nestle in stems of fall leaves and berries and let them trail onto the table. Nothing is glued into the bowl, so you can use everything again. The key is to keep the design light and airy. Play with the branches until they look natural.

A lightweight throw ties the colors together and adds softness. Throws, shawls, and scarves are colorful alternatives to traditional table linens.

ELEMENTS

Lightweight fabric throw, shawl, or scarf in warm colors

Large wooden bowl

Faux pomegranates and mangoes, enough to fill the bowl abundantly

Three long branches of faux fall leaves with berries

PUTTING IT TOGETHER

1   Place the fabric in the center of the table. Swish it into an S shape, with the ends pointing toward the ends of the table. Scrunch it up so the look is loose and casual.

2   Place the bowl on top of the throw. Set six pieces of fruit aside and fill the bowl with the rest, rearranging until you are happy with the look.

3   Curl the ends of the branches and nestle the branches among the fruits. Trail the ends out of the bowl and along the table.

4   Casually place the remaining fruit next to the bowl as shown.

ADAPTATIONS

- When fall turns into winter, pop in a couple of wispy pine branches and the design is ready for a new season.

- Holiday collectables, such as a Santa or angels, can be added and moved at mealtime.

Candlescape with Magnolias

This elegant design is amazingly easy to make. You can turn any tray into the base for a candlescape—a "landscape" of pillar candles in different heights. The candles pictured have an interesting birch-bark texture, but you can also use plain cream-colored ones. Faux floral stems are just woven through the candles—no glue! Their beautiful stems are an important part of the design.

A hammered bronze tray and magnolias create a warm, rich look for fall-to-winter. The colors add lightness to dark wood furniture and contrast nicely with light furniture. A big, floppy, satin bow provides a lush look and reflects the candlelight beautifully. The double-faced satin ribbon is especially gorgeous, and the butterscotch color complements the bronze and magnolia.

Changing the florals and ribbon can easily restyle the piece from fall through the holidays to winter. Be sure to replace the candles when they burn down and get near the florals.

ELEMENTS

Hammered bronze tray

Sheet of dry floral foam, 2" (5 cm) thick

Marker

Putty knife

Duct tape, optional

Glue gun

Block of dry floral foam

Knife

Spoon

Five medium and tall pillar candles, cream colored

Sheet moss

River rocks in a variety of natural colors

One magnolia leaf garland, 30" (76 cm) long

Four stems of faux magnolia flowers

Two stems of bittersweet

4 ft. (1.23 m) satin ribbon

Two pieces floral wire for tying bows

1½ yd. (1.4 m) sheer fabric, 18" (46 cm) wide

PUTTING IT TOGETHER

1   Place sheet foam on a work surface and place the tray on top. Using a marker, draw the outline. Cut out the foam with a putty knife. Secure the foam to the bottom of the tray with hot glue. If you prefer, apply duct tape to the bottom of the tray and secure the foam to the tape.

2   Cut the block of foam in half; trim off the corners. Glue the block in the center of the foam in the tray. Place your candle on top of the block, and mark around it. With the knife, cut a hole 2" (5 cm) deep. Scoop out the foam with a spoon. Insert one of the tall candles.

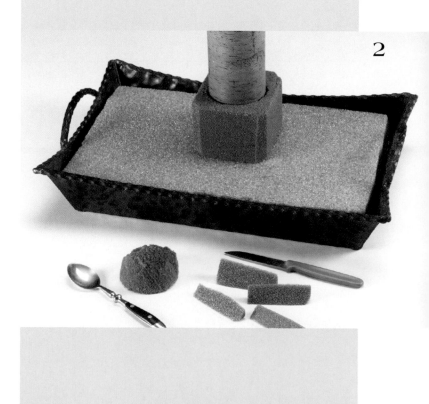

3　Arrange the other candles on the foam, be random rather than too symmetrical, and vary the heights and placements. Draw around each candle with a marker. Remove the candles and cut holes in the foam, 1" (2.5 cm) deep. Push the candles into the holes.

4　Cover the foam with sheet moss. Glue the moss down near the edges. Sprinkle river rocks over the moss.

5　Weave the magnolia leaf garland through the candles.

6　Twist two magnolia flower stems and a bittersweet stem together. Bend them into an S shape. Curl the ends around your hand. Repeat with another set.

7　Place the stems gently between the candles in opposite directions.

8　Cut the ribbon in half and make two loose bows (see page 12). Tuck the bows into the garlands, hiding the wire.

9　Arrange the sheer fabric on the table. Tie large knots in the ends. Place the tray on top.

ADAPTATIONS

• To change the design for the holidays, remove the bittersweet and add a few ornaments or a beaded garland.

• Use the candlescape without adding any florals.

• Replace the magnolia garland with fresh lemon leaves on long stems.

Feathers with Seasonal Branches

A VERSATILE VASE ARRANGEMENT

Feathers provide a stylish decorating accent. In this dramatic vase design, the feathers form the base for arrangements that can be easily adapted to fit the season.

Because of its size, this is not the kind of centerpiece that makes it possible to talk across a table. It is better suited for the dining room that is used only occasionally. Also, many people like to have a showpiece to decorate a table that's not always used for dining. This arrangement can be easily moved to a sideboard when you want to use the table.

Long exotic pheasant feathers like these are available from florist shops or interior design centers. Shorter feathers can be lengthened with floral wire.

ELEMENTS

Regal clear glass vase, 12" to 14" (30.5 to 61 cm) tall and a bit wider at the top than bottom

River rocks

Pheasant feathers, 3 ft. (1 m) long or extended to that length with wire

20-gauge wire

Brown floral tape

Several seasonal branches, 3 ft. (1 m) long

PUTTING IT TOGETHER

1   Carefully place river rocks into the vase until it is about one-half to three-fourths full.

2   Extend feathers to 3 ft. (1 m), if necessary, by placing a wire alongside the lower part of the feather shaft. Wrap the wire and feather together with floral tape. To join two or more feathers on one stem, wire and tape each feather first. Then add them in, one at a time, as you wrap down the main stem.

3   Put the feathers into the vase, pushing the ends a few inches into the rock. Arrange them so they flare out over the top of the vase.

2

4   Cut seasonal branches 3 ft. (1 m) long or the same length as the feathers. Add them to the vase, pushing them into the rocks.

5   Adjust the arrangement so the branches hide the wire extenders.

VARIATIONS In the spring, you can switch the branches to pussy willows. In the winter, red ilex berry branches are spectacular (as shown below). Yellow orchid stems are breathtaking in the summer.

ADAPTATIONS

- You can replace the rocks with a dry filler, such as pumpkin pods, apple pods, juniper berries, cut bamboo shoots, or evergreen twigs. Be careful though, since the vase will not be weighted as well and may tip over if it is bumped. You can start with a layer of rock to add more stability.

- Replace the glass vase with a ceramic or metal urn; golden brown would look great with the brown feathers.

A Garland for Harvest to Holidays

TUCKING SEASONAL BUNDLES
INTO A BEADED FRUIT GARLAND

A garland becomes an instant centerpiece when you form it into an S shape and place candlesticks in the curves.

This version starts with two splendid garlands, one of glossy, burgundy magnolia leaves and the other of sparkling beaded fruits. Rose bouquets form the special accent. Once you have created this basic centerpiece, you can easily make seasonal changes by replacing the accents. In fall, use bundles of berries and feathers. Then move into the holidays with rose bouquets and gold ribbon.

ELEMENTS

Garland of faux
magnolia leaves

Garland of beaded fruit

Three or four black cable
ties or floral wire

Pair of candlesticks

Candles

Nine large faux emerging
roses in pale orange

Wire cutters

Floral tape

3 yd. (2.75 m) sheer
copper-colored wire-edge
ribbon, 3" (7.5 cm) wide

PUTTING IT TOGETHER

1   Lay the magnolia garland down the
    center of your table. Lay the beaded
    fruit garland on top. Join the garlands
    together in a few places with cable
    ties, hiding them in the leaves. (White
    ties were used for visibility.)

2   Bunch and curve the garlands into a
    loose S shape.

3   Place the candlesticks in the curves
    of the S, up against the garlands.
    Add the candles.

4   Make three rose bouquets, each with
    two or three roses. Wrap the stems
    together with floral tape. Tuck the
    roses into the garlands.

5   Cut the ribbon in half. From each
    length, make one large floppy bow,
    as shown on page 12. Insert the
    bows into the garland as shown.

VARIATION For fall, bunch three short pheasant feathers with picks of orange ashberry and secure with several twists of wire toward the bottom of the pick. Cover the wire and the bottom half of the stem with floral tape. Tuck the bunches into the garlands.

ADAPTATIONS

- Take the design into early spring by changing the accents to small bunches of preserved ferns wired together.

- Replace the beaded fruit with wide ribbon.

- Put a throw or an elegant shawl under the centerpiece.

A DISPLAY OF FAVORITE ORNAMENTS

You can turn opulent Christmas ornaments into an instant centerpiece. Choose special balls with various textures and similar colors. Arrange them in a pedestal container, and soften the design by draping on a bead garland. This small centerpiece leaves lots of room on your table for a holiday meal. You can add candlesticks and a table runner.

ELEMENTS

Pedestal display stand, candy dish, or cake stand

Special holiday ball ornaments in similar tones

Bead garland, 1 yd. (1 m) long

PUTTING IT TOGETHER

1   Place the pedestal dish in the center of the table.

2   Arrange the ornaments in a mound, putting different styles next to each other. Tuck under any loops on the ornaments, so you can use the ornaments on a tree later.

3   Put one end of the bead garland in the center of the arrangement. Drape the garland over and around the ornaments and off the edge of the container here and there. Tuck the other end back into the center. You do not need to secure the garland; just be careful when moving the design.

3

- For a large table, use three pedestal containers with ornaments.

- Add candlesticks. With the design in the photograph, gold, plum, or burgundy candles would be gorgeous.

- Reuse the bead garland for another centerpiece by laying it on top of a faux or fresh evergreen garland. You can even weave in battery-operated white holiday lights.

Entertaining

Asian Simplicity

ORCHIDS AND BAMBOO
CANDLEHOLDERS

T his serene centerpiece is perfect for entertaining with a Japanese, Thai, or Chinese menu. With its clean, simple lines, it can be a lasting part of the décor of a contemporary or transitional home.

Red is a popular color in Asia, but you can use any color that works in the room. Choose the vases first, then select orchids and candles in the same color for a harmonious look.

This design features an unusual candleholder—a length of bamboo. Bamboo is available in craft stores and from your local florist. It is surprisingly easy to split, especially if you pick a piece that already has a crack.

ELEMENTS

Natural color rattan runner

Three small Asian style vases

Three stems faux oncidium orchids

Three sticks of pan reed (sold in a bundle)

4-ft. (1.25 m) piece of bamboo, preferably with a crack

Hacksaw, if needed

Kitchen knife (dull)

Craft sand, natural color

Ten tea lights, same color as the vases or orchids

PUTTING IT TOGETHER

1   Place the runner down the center of your table.

2   Arrange the vases, evenly spaced, in a straight line down the middle of the runner.

3   Place an orchid stem in each vase. Shape and curve the stems so they mirror each other, as shown. Add a reed to each vase.

4   Lay the bamboo on a work surface. If the bamboo is too long for your table, cut it with a hacksaw. Insert the knife in the crack and apply pressure until the bamboo splits down the middle.

3

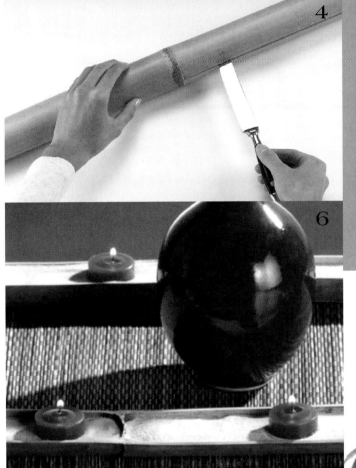

4

6

ADAPTATIONS

- Replace the bamboo with filled-glass votives.

- Place flower heads from a stem of cymbidium orchid at the ends of the bamboo.

- Use colored sand.

5 Place one piece of the bamboo, hollow side up, on each side of the vases. Adjust them so one is slightly further to the right, the other slightly further to the left. Fill each half full with sand to steady it and provide a base for the candles.

6 Arrange the candles evenly in the bamboo.

Hot Colors, Hot Peppers

ELEMENTS FOR
A MENU WITH HEAT

When you're hosting a dinner party with ethnic food, let the menu inspire the centerpiece. This design captures the fun, colors, and spicy foods of Mexico, Latin America, or the Caribbean.

Take your color cues from a bright table runner or cloth. Most of the elements for this centerpiece can be picked up when you're shopping for the food. Look for ideas in the international foods aisle. Import stores are another good source; that's where I found these inexpensive spice jars. Filled with a variety of dried beans and peas, the jars become small vases for flowers that dance along your table. The finishing touch is a scattering of hot peppers from the produce section.

Without the fresh peppers, this centerpiece makes a wonderful summer arrangement, especially for Southwestern or contemporary décor. This design would also look great in an informal kitchen dining area.

ELEMENTS

Colorful runner, throw, or tablecloth

About six spice jars or small bottles

Small dried beans and peas in several colors

One small stem of bright faux florals for each jar; four orange meadow daisies and two yellow poppies were used here

Wire cutters

Several fresh hot peppers (the small ones) in variety of colors

PUTTING IT TOGETHER

1   Place the runner or cloth down the center of the table. If you are using a cloth, bunch it up casually and tie the ends in loose knots.

2   Fill the jars with beans and peas.

3   Cut the flower stems about 9" (23 cm) long with wire cutters. Place one in each bottle. Bend and twist the stems for movement and to create a natural look.

4   Scatter the peppers on the cloth.

4

ADAPTATIONS

- To use fresh flowers, insert each stem into a water tube before placing it into the bean-filled jar. Or, instead of beans, fill the jars with water tinted with a few drops of food coloring.

- Instead of scattering the peppers, put them in a low, clear-glass bowl or a piece of Mexican or Southwestern pottery.

- Add small votive candles down the table.

- If you use different flowers, choose ones with small heads so they don't overwhelm the vases. Zinnias would be great.

Radicchio and Ivy

GARDEN DESIGN WITH VEGETABLE VASES

This fresh garden design adds a spectacular focal point for a dinner party or other special event and can be created at any time of the year. The container is an iron urn from the garden center. Pick up some small rocks for the bottom of the urn in the garden store or your craft store.

The flower vases are hollowed-out radicchio, a purplish-red leafy vegetable. You may have seen gourds and pumpkins used as flower containers, but radicchio is something unique. It has a marvelous color and texture, and unlike cabbage, it doesn't have a strong smell. You can prepare the vases hours before the event. Later, remove them and you have a nice ivy plant to enjoy inside or out. Ivy likes sunlight, so if you want to keep the arrangement on a table away from light for a long time, use faux ivy instead.

An advantage of using fresh produce in your centerpiece is that you can pick up the elements when you're buying groceries. A small ivy plant, a few veggies, a bouquet of tulips, and you're in business.

ELEMENTS

White iron urn

Small rocks for the bottom of the urn

Potting soil

Small ivy plant

Three heads radicchio

Sharp kitchen knife

Spoon

Three shot glasses or glass votive holders

About a dozen white tulips

Baby's breath

PUTTING IT TOGETHER

1   Put a layer of small rocks in the bottom of the urn. Fill the urn with potting soil and plant the ivy in the center. Water as needed.

2   In the center of each head of radicchio, cut a hole large enough to hold the small votive or shot glass, going all the way to the bottom. Scoop out the center with a spoon. Insert the glass.

4

ADAPTATIONS

- Create a faux version by inserting faux ivy, kale, and tulips into dry floral foam.

- For a fall look, insert the glasses into a split acorn squash and fill with ashberry clumps; add fall leaves around the edge of the container.

- For a winter look, fill the urn with evergreen and red ilex berries.

3   Place the radicchio into the arrangement as shown. Fill the glasses with water.

4   Cut the tulips at an angle so the stems are about 3" (7.5 cm) long and place them immediately into the "vases."

5   Cut the baby's breath into short bunches. Insert them into the design around the tulips.

6   Place the design on your table.

Your Special
Serving Piece

TUREEN OR BOWL ON A BED OF COLOR

What treasures do you have hidden away in your china cabinet or boxed in the attic? Many of us have a large tureen or painted serving bowl that has been passed down in the family. If you do, consider giving it a place of honor at your holiday or family gathering.

Dress up the bowl or tureen by putting it on a tray and adding fresh produce. Choose foods that bring out the colors of the serving piece. Shown here is a Thanksgiving centerpiece with glossy brown chestnuts, orange kumquats, and green Brussels sprouts. Complete the design with a length of fabric that brings out the colors of the serving piece.

ELEMENTS

Large, covered tureen or decorative serving bowl

Tray several inches wider than the tureen or bowl

Length of soft, drapable fabric

Chestnuts or other nuts in the shell

Kumquats and Brussels sprouts, or other small, fresh, colorful produce

PUTTING IT TOGETHER

1 Wash the tureen or bowl and place it on the tray.

2 Arrange the fabric lengthwise on the table, in soft folds and ripples. Center the bowl and tray on top.

3 Cover the tray with a mixture of chestnuts and fresh produce.

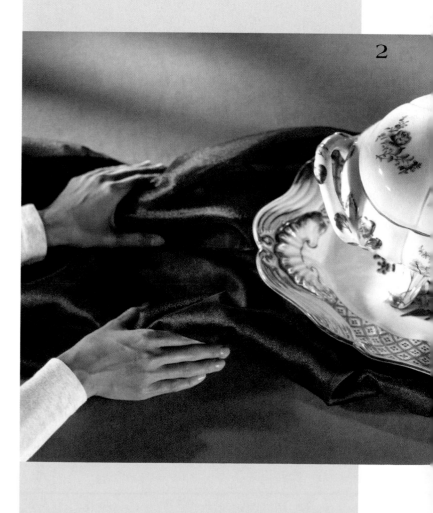

86

VARIATION *If you are using a serving piece that has no lid, fill the bowl with one full bunch of fresh, fragrant, seeded eucalyptus from the florist. Cut fresh floral foam to fit the bowl, soak it in water, and place it in the bowl. Cover it with green sheet moss. Cut the eucalyptus into short stems. Starting at the edges, insert stems to form a low, round mound.*

ADAPTATIONS

- Use a gold or silver bowl and tray.

- Use different nuts, fruits, and vegetables.

- You can also serve soup or other dishes from the bowl or tureen; the design becomes the focal point of your buffet.

Champagne
and Roses

ROMANTIC DINNER FOR TWO

This design is perfect for a table for two—for a date, an anniversary, Valentine's Day, or just to say "I love you." You can use whatever small tray and wine or champagne holder you have, though inexpensive silvered ones like the one used here would be a romantic gift. Use the tray later to pass hors d'ouevres at a party—or use it the next morning to serve breakfast in bed! A red napkin is included in the design; you may want to purchase three, so you have two to go with the place settings.

ELEMENTS

Small silver tray

Silver champagne bucket or similar silver container

Seven short stems of faux large white rosebuds

Floral tape

2 ft. (0.63 m) sheer white ribbon

Scissors

Red cloth napkin

Newspaper

Several sheets white tissue paper

Champagne bottle

Three red filled-glass votives or glass holders and candles

PUTTING IT TOGETHER

1 Place the champagne bucket to the back of the tray.

2 Crumple newspaper and put it in the bottom of the bucket to hold the champagne bottle high in the bucket. Cover the newspaper with some tissue paper. Place the champagne bottle on top, angling it to the side.

3 Cut the stems of the roses 5" (12.7 cm) long with wire cutters. Hold them together to form a small bouquet, and secure temporarily with a few wraps of floral tape. Wrap the stems with ribbon and tie a bow.

4 Drape the napkin over the edge of the bucket on the side opposite the bottle. Place the bouquet on the napkin, angled to the side.

5 Place the votives on the tray in front of the arrangement, making sure that the ribbon and napkin are away from the candle flame.

ADAPTATIONS

- Use small fresh roses with a water tube or put them in a glass of water if it fits into the space.

- Tie a small key into the bouquet to say that the person holds the key to your heart.

- Sprinkle silk or fresh rose petals on the tray.

- Set a small tied bouquet next to candlesticks on the table for a simple but romantic centerpiece.

Tea and Pearls

TEACUPS AND A PEARL
GARLAND

This charming centerpiece for a tea, brunch, luncheon, or shower is as ladylike and classic as a string of pearls.

The base is a loose S-shaped lemon-leaf garland. Teacups tucked into the curves hold aromatic tea and floating candles. The teacups need not match—in fact the design is more interesting if they don't.

You can save money by cutting apart flowers sold as a bush and tucking them into the garland. The flowers don't need to be glued in place because the centerpiece is intended for a special occasion rather than as a lasting decoration. The cream pearl garland draped on top is the perfect finishing touch and can be found in the wedding section of a craft store.

The design shown here looks beautiful on a white, cream, light green, or soft watermelon tablecloth.

ELEMENTS

Two faux lemon-leaf garlands, 4 to 6 ft. (1.23 to 1.85 m) long

Two bushes faux watermelon-colored begonias

Wire cutters

Pearl garland

Floral wire

Green floral tape

Three teacups and saucers

Brewed tea

Three white floating candles

PUTTING IT TOGETHER

1   Curve one of the lemon-leaf garlands into an S shape on the table. Lay the second garland next to it and overlapping.

2   With the wire cutters, cut the bushes into individual stems at least 3" (7.5 cm) long, each with a flower or two and leaves.

3   Tuck the flowers into the garland.

4   Drape the pearl garland over the lemon-leaf garland.

5   Place the teacups in the curves of the garland.

6   Pour fragrant tea into the cups, and float the candles.

2

3

ADAPTATIONS

- Substitute fresh lemon-leaf stems, also called salal leaves, for the faux garlands.

- If you insert the flowers without wire or glue, you can remove and replace them for other events or seasons—orange berries or red leaves for fall, evergreens and festive red ribbon for the holidays.

- Place small holiday ornamental balls in small crystal bowls in the curves of the lemon garland for an elegant Christmas look.

- Nestle candlesticks in the curves of the garland for everyday use.

- For a special event, use single fresh roses in water tubes.

4

Dinner at Eight

ORCHIDS, IVY, AND CRYSTAL

Create an elegant atmosphere for your next dinner party with this posh but easy to make centerpiece.

The look begins with stunning orchids. Choose high-quality florals with attractive stems that become part of your design. This design looks fabulous against a pale peach tablecloth, but you could also put the florals directly on a wood tabletop.

The design features soft candlelight to set the mood. Stemware candleholders provide an unusual and witty touch. Choose any stemware or crystal that flares out at the top. When you buy the candles, take a glass along to check the fit. You could use votives, but the small floating candles have a round, interesting form.

The candles are set on bath salts that form a safe base and add sparkle. Choose salts with a subtle fragrance. Alternatively, fill the glasses with water and float the candles.

Ivy garland,
5 ft. (1.58 m) long

Three cymbidium orchids
with long stems

Five stemmed glasses

White bath salts

Five small floating
candles or votives

PUTTING IT TOGETHER

1   Arrange the ivy down the center of
the table in soft curves.

2   Curl the stems of the orchids around
your hand. Lay them in three places
along the ivy, pointing in different
directions. Leave some space
between them.

3   Place the glasses next to the garland,
spaced somewhat evenly apart on
alternating sides. Put bath salts in
each glass with a candle on top.

3

ADAPTATIONS

- Choose candles that are white, the color of the orchids, or the color of your décor.

- Replace the stemware with glass candlesticks of varied heights.

- For coordinated place settings, slip napkins into rings and tuck a short orchid stem into each one.

- Use small, clear rocks instead of the bath salts.

Sweet Spring Arbor

TIERED SERVER FOR A SPRING EVENT

An arch of flowering branches is a dramatic and pretty centerpiece for a spring occasion, such as Easter, a bridal or baby shower, or a brunch. An arbor is formed by winding supple, flowering branches, such as faux bleeding heart, up the legs and over the handle of a tiered server. Cracked halves of eggshells add enchanting details and a traditional spring accent. You can use faux eggshells sold in several colors in craft stores or make your own. Fill the top of the server with pastel candy almonds or other treats.

ELEMENTS

Two-tiered fruit or vegetable basket or serving piece

Sheet moss

Three stems faux bleeding heart, each 3 ft. (0.92 m) long

Twelve faux eggshell halves, or six brown eggs cracked in half and cleaned

Several faux quail eggs

Bunny garden accent or other spring accessory

Pastel candy-coated almonds or other candy

PUTTING IT TOGETHER

1 Place the tiered serving piece in the center of the table. Put the bunny or other accessory in the middle of the bottom layer of the server.

2 If you don't have faux eggshell halves, crack six raw eggs in two. Wash the shells thoroughly and allow to dry.

3 Fill each shell half with a bit of sheet moss. Arrange the eggshells around the bunny. Add quail eggs here and there.

4 Fill the upper tier with candy-coated almonds or other candy.

5 Twist the bleeding heart stems up the legs and around the handle of the serving piece, trailing the ends onto the table.

3

5

ADAPTATIONS

• Replace the eggshells with painted or dyed Easter eggs.

• Fill the upper tier with cookies or petit fours.

• If you can start a couple weeks ahead, you can have fresh grass in your design. Fill the shells with potting soil, sprinkle on wheat berry seeds, place in the sun, water often, and watch the grass grow.

Watermelon

A NATURAL CONTAINER FOR FRESH FLOWERS

A watermelon is mostly water, so why not use it as the "vase" for flowers? This bright centerpiece is perfect for a buffet table at a casual outdoor party. Consider it for a graduation party, a neighborhood July 4th celebration, and other summer events. Imagine this design surrounded by bowls of salads and fresh fruits.

Choose casual, bright flowers like these sunflowers. Stick to flowers in a single color, so the design doesn't look too busy. Make sure you have enough flowers to cover the top of the melon.

An old picnic basket—the more worn and battered, the better—is a charming container for this design. If you use a tablecloth, consider green or melon color.

ELEMENTS

Watermelon

About 10 stems of sunflowers or other large, bright flowers

Large picnic basket

Clay pot, 6" to 8" (15 to 20.5 cm) diameter

Small garden statue

Grape garland with grapes

PUTTING IT TOGETHER

1   Slice off one end of the watermelon, and eat or discard the end. The cut surface becomes the top of the "vase."

2   Prop the watermelon in a bowl to keep it upright while you add the flowers. Cut the stems of the flowers 7" (18 cm) long at an angle. Insert them in the watermelon until the surface is covered.

3   Place the clay pot into the picnic basket to one side. Prop the watermelon upright in the pot.

4   Place the garden statue next to the watermelon.

5   Wind the grape garland around the statue, filling in the empty spaces in the basket and trailing out onto the table.

ADAPTATIONS

- Scoop out all of the watermelon to serve your guests and fill the the hollow rind with water to hold a bouquet of flowers.

- Cut a lengthwise slice from a watermelon and use the rest to make a low, horizontal floral arrangement. Add an ivy garland around the base and trail it toward the sides.

- Make a low mounded floral arrangement in the small watermelon cap. Use daisies or zinnias for a different look.

Tropical Beach

OUTDOOR FUN

Bring a tropical beach to your backyard for a summer get-together. A beach, Caribbean, or luau theme is popular with all ages and for many occasions, including graduations and even weddings. The hot pinks, reds, and bright greens are very festive. Paper and plastic party ware comes in bright tropical colors and designs to complete the table. Don't forget the blender for the tropical drinks!

The cost is low. You need only two stems of faux tropical florals and four leaves, all of which you can reuse later. Use shells from a beach vacation (so this is why you've been saving them!) or buy a bag at your craft store. The bamboo candle stake is sold in craft and garden stores.

This centerpiece is perfect for a long buffet table, but you can dine around it, too. The elements are tall enough for your guests to see below them across the table.

ELEMENTS

Four faux taro leaves
with long stems

Raffia

Galvanized tin bucket

Craft or garden sand,
enough to fill the bucket

Two faux exotic stems,
such as heliconia
lobster claw and scarlet
star bromeliad

Shells

Bamboo candle stake
about 3 ft. (1 m) high

Candle, citronella or
regular

Two or more medium-
sized glass candle-
holders and candles in
tropical colors

PUTTING IT TOGETHER

1   Lay the taro leaves face up along the center of the table, two leaves pointing each way and the stems bundled together. Adjust the stems so the larger leaves extend further out. Wrap the stems together with raffia.

2   Fill the bucket with sand to 2" (5 cm) from the top. Place the bucket on the table.

3   Place the candle stake deep into the sand and angled to one side. Insert the exotic stems into the sand. Make sure the florals will not be near the candle flame.

4   Place some shells on the sand and scatter others along the table.

5   Place candleholders near the bucket for more candlelight.

- For an inside party, put a regular candle in a glass container into the candle stake or omit that element and put more candleholders on the table. Do not use citronella candles inside.

- Use any exotic florals; red ginger is also a great look.

- Add orchid stems on top of the leaves.

- Create matching centerpieces for small dining tables by placing one exotic leaf on the table and topping it with a matching candleholder and seashells.

- Place faux orchid heads into the shells. If the shells hold water, use fresh orchids.

Index